DINOSAURS ALIVE!

Get set for the dinosaur book [...] prehistoric giants, such as Ty[...] and Stegosaurus, roaring bac[...]

D0674319

Dinosaurs Alive uses augmented reality (AR) technology to set loose a range of awesome dinosaurs and send them stomping across these pages in jaw-dropping 3D. Here's what to do…

1  Check that your computer has a **webcam** and that it can run the augmented reality (AR) software on your installation disc (see the **Minimum System Requirements** panel opposite).

2  Put the **installation disc** into your computer and double-click on the installer software. Then follow the on-screen instructions to install the software on your hard drive and start the program.

3  As you go through the book, look out for this symbol which shows you're on a **special AR page**. Once you see that the software is running, hold the page in front of your webcam. Now watch your dinosaur come to life!

TOP DINO-WATCHING TIPS

 Look out for special keys you can press to open the crates and make your dinosaurs run, roar and attack.

 For a different angle, try turning or tilting the page, or hold it nearer the webcam to get really close!

 To view full screen, click the green button on the AR window. To close the window, click the red cross.

 For the best dinosaur animation experience, avoid having too much light reflecting off the page.

 Make sure your computer speakers are turned up loud!

Need some help?

If you've got a problem, check out our website for troubleshooting information:

www.carltonbooks.co.uk

Credits

The publishers would like to thank the following sources for their kind permission to reproduce the pictures in this book.

Photograph indicators: *t* – top, *b* – bottom, *l* – left, *r* – right, *c* – centre

Pages are numbered as follows: Front endpaper 2–3; Credits and title pages 4–5; Meet the Dinosaurs 6–7; Old Timers 8–9; Super Heavyweights 10–11; Diplodocus 12–13; Flesh-eating Killing Machines 14–15; Micro Monsters 16–17; Tough Guys 18–19; Stegosaurus 20–21; Sprinters and Plodders 22–23; Scary Oddballs 24–25; Quetzalcoatlus 26–27; Ferocious Beasts 28–29; Power Packs 30–31; Big Heads 32–33; Pentaceratops 34–35; The Longest and the Tallest 36–37; Masterminds 38–39; Extreme Eaters 40–41; Tyrannosaurus 42–43; Death and Extinction 44–45; Glossary and quiz answers 46–47

Every effort has been made to acknowledge correctly and contact the source and/or copyright holder of each picture and Carlton Books Limited apologizes for any unintentional errors or omissions which will be corrected in future editions of this book.

PICTURE CREDITS

American Museum of Natural History: A.E.Anderson: 33*b*; **Alamy Images:** Nick Ayliffe: 45*br*; **Ardea:** Adrian Warren: 9*cr*; **Corbis:** Theo Allofs: 23*t*, /Jonathan Blair: 24, /DK Images: 37, /DK Images/Colin Keates: 44*bl*, /Sandy Felsenthal: 10*tl*, /Louie Psihoyos: 17*t*, 17*b*, 32*bl*, 36*b*, 40*t*, /Reuters: 25, /Kevin Schafer: 32*c*, /Jim Sugar: 45*r*; **DK Images:** 7, 41*bl*; **FLPA:** Simon Liffen: 33*tr*, /Minden Pictures: 11, /Martin B Withers: 37*b*; **Getty Images:** Theo Allofs: 9*br*, /Brian Jaquest: 12, /Louie Psihoyos: 11*cl*, 16*bl*, 36*c*, /Valerie Shaff: 34, /Art Wolfe: 36*t*; **Masterfile:** Londolozi: 18*b*; **NHPA:** Anthony Bannister: 9*tr*; **Natural History Museum, London:** 6–7, 16–17, 19*br*, 20, 23*r*, 38, 40*b*; **Hannah Porter:** 12 (inset figures); **Photolibrary. com:** Fabio Colombini Medeiras: 19*tr*, /Pat Canova: 42, /Mark MacEwen: 44*b*; **Senckenberg Research Institute an Natural History Museum, Frankfurt/M. (Germany):** 26; **Steve Bloom Images:** 22*tr*, 31, 40*br*, 45*bl*

Published in 2010 by Carlton Books Limited
An imprint of the Carlton Publishing Group
20 Mortimer Street
London W1T 3JW

A catalogue record for this book is available from the British Library.

ISBN: 978-1-84732-578-5

Consultants: Peter Andrews and Roger Benson
Art director: Russell Porter
Executive editor: Barry Timms
Editor: Honor Head
Editorial director: Jane Wilsher
Picture research: Rebecca Sodergren and Steve Behan
Production: Claire Hayward

DANGER! this book really bites back!

In memory of Ben Cook, for whom dinosaurs were very much alive

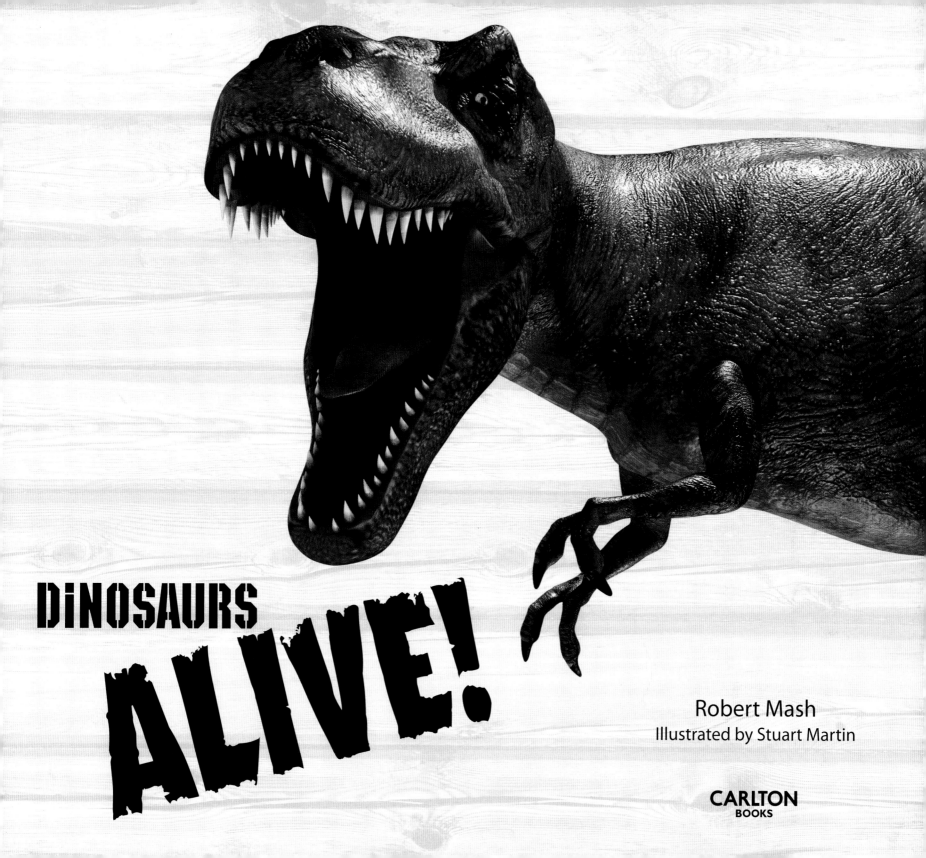

DINOSAURS
ALIVE!

Robert Mash

Illustrated by Stuart Martin

CARLTON
BOOKS

Meet the DINOSAURS

Among the most incredible creatures ever to walk the Earth, the dinosaurs ruled our world for more than 160 million years.

Examining the Evidence

Dead dinosaurs usually rotted away or were eaten. Tough parts like bones, teeth and claws sometimes hardened to stone and have been preserved as fossils.

Bones tell us about the size and shape of an animal. Teeth and claws give us clues about what the animals ate. Tracks of their footprints give us an idea of their size and how they moved.

By piecing all these clues together, paleontologists (scientists who study prehistoric life) can begin to understand how the dinosaurs lived.

THE DINOSAUR DYNASTY

At the beginning of the Triassic period, about 250 million years ago (mya), there were two main groups of land reptiles, the synapsids (the most numerous) and the archosaurs. However, by the end of the Triassic, about 203 million years ago, the archosaurs had taken over. These reptiles included the crocodiles, the pterosaurs and the dinosaurs.

Compared with the synapsids, the dinosaurs were extreme in almost every way – bigger, fiercer and faster! By the beginning of the Jurassic period the synapsids had seen off nearly all the rival land creatures. The only other large animals were the marine reptiles, such as the plesiosaurs, and the pterosaurs who ruled the skies.

Skin Deep

We can't know what colours dinosaurs were, but by looking at animals today we can make good guesses. Dinosaurs would have been coloured either for camouflage or with striking patterns to attract mates or ward off rivals. Their skins were usually leathery, with bumps or knobs.

The Age of Dinosaurs

Conifers, ginkgos and seed ferns were common. Reptiles and amphibians were widespread. The first dinosaurs, crocodiles and pterosaurs appeared. The first mammals appeared.	Cycads, conifers and ferns flourished. The first birds appeared. DINOSAURS RULED! Marine reptiles and pterosaurs took many forms.	The first flowering plants appeared. Conifers flourished, cycads and ginkgos were less common. Dinosaurs remained the dominant land animals but died out at the end of the Cretaceous period. Small mammals became widespread.
TRIASSIC PERIOD	**JURASSIC PERIOD**	**CRETACEOUS PERIOD**

← **MESOZOIC ERA: 250–65 MILLION YEARS AGO** →

250 million years ago **203** mya **135** mya **65** my

Brachiosaurus
(BRACK-ee-oh-SORE-us)

LIVED: 150–140 mya

PERIOD: Jurassic

LOCALITY: USA and Tanzania

LENGTH: 23 m (75 ft)

HEIGHT: 13 m (42 ½ ft)

WEIGHT: Up to 80 tonnes

DIET: Herbivore – ate plants

EXTREME SUCCESS!

Why did the dinosaurs come to dominate the planet for such a long period of time? Their body structures evolved to make them fast and agile, which gave them an edge over their competitors. Some scientists believe that dinosaurs were warm-blooded, which means they were able to keep their temperatures at the same level. This would have allowed for a more active lifestyle and a bigger, more efficient brain.

There were very many different kinds of dinosaurs. Some were enormous, like *Argentinosaurus,* and some were small, like *Coelophysis*. Some were active, like *Velociraptor,* and some were sluggish, like *Euoplocephalus*. The dinosaurs in this book are the ones we know about now, but new fossil discoveries are being made all the time…

The Body Beautiful

What features allowed the early dinosaurs to out-run, out-fight and out-eat their competitors?

- Straight legs, tucked under the body

- A long tail for balance, which meant that some could run on only two legs

- Grasping hands to grab hold of their prey

- More powerful jaw muscles, for better chewing

- Lighter and stronger bones

lungs

spines on vertebrae (for muscle attachment)

neck muscles

LEFT: *Brachiosaurus* is a good example of how later dinosaurs adapted to their environment. Instead of grasping hands, it has sturdy feet to support its massive body. Its gizzard (a muscular stomach to break up food) aids digestion, and it has a big heart to pump blood up to its head.

LEFT: The fossilized knobbly skin of one of the armoured dinosaurs, *Polacanthus*.

heart   gizzard

stout legs with sturdy feet

long tail (to balance neck)

Old TiMERS

During the Triassic period, the most amazing creatures ever were taking over the world.

THE ANCiENT EARTH

Throughout the Triassic period the climate was dry and warm, and because there were no large inland seas or polar ice-caps, the temperatures were constant. At this time there were no flowering plants. In the drier parts of the planet there were conifer trees like redwoods, cypresses and monkey puzzles, as well as less familiar trees like cycads and podocarps. In moister places and near rivers there were tree ferns, club mosses and horsetails.

ABOVE: Fossil finds show that _Plateosaurus_ was the largest early plant-eating dinosaur.

THE FiRST DiNOSAURS

The first of the dinosaurs appeared in the middle Triassic period, 230 to 225 million years ago. We know that the basic design of the dinosaurs helped them to become successful. But apart from their mobility and speed, what else might have given them the edge? Why did dinosaurs beat other animals in the race to the top?

It may be that in the dry and hot conditions, the early dinosaurs' reptilian waterproof skin was better at preventing them from drying out than the fur coats of the early mammals. Whatever the reason, dinosaurs came to dominate – mammals had to wait for nearly 150 million years for their chance to shine!

RIGHT: All continents were once joined to form a single land mass.

Moving Continents

During the Triassic period Earth's land mass was was one enormous supercontinent called Pangaea.

Towards the end of the Jurassic period, the northern part of Pangaea had drifted away from the southern part. They formed two new supercontinents – Laurasia in the north and Gondwana in the south – separated by the Tethys Ocean.

By the end of the Cretaceous period, 150 million years later, the land had moved again and formed the continents much as we know them today.

Lean and Mean

Coelophysis is one of the best-known examples of an early dinosaur. About 3 m (10 ft) long, it was a lean, mean two-legged meat-eater. It used grasping claws to capture its victims, and sharp, pointed teeth to devour them. Its teeth would not have been much good at chewing, however, so *Coelophysis* swallowed its prey in huge chunks.

RIGHT: *Coelophysis*, a well-known early dinosaur, shows off the two straight back legs that helped to make the dinosaurs so hugely dominant.

ABOVE: *Proterosuchus*, a primitive archosaur, had a sprawling leg position, like today's crocodile (above right).

ABOVE RIGHT: *Euparkeria* had "semi-improved" legs, more upright than those of *Proterosuchus*. The modern-day Komodo dragon (above left) has the same leg position.

GETTING BETTER AND BETTER

What do we know about the evolution of the first dinosaurs? It is likely that an early archosaur, such as *Proterosuchus*, evolved into an animal with "semi-improved" legs (legs that were more upright), rather like *Euparkeria*. This little reptile was usually sprawled on its belly, but it could raise itself up and run on its back legs. The next stage was the evolution of "true" dinosaurs, with straight back legs underneath the body, like the early *Herrerasaurus*.

Large prosauropods such as *Plateosaurus* appeared around the same time. These plant-eaters grew to 8 m (26 ft) in length. They were tall enough to reach food at the tops of trees that smaller dinosaurs couldn't reach and being big helped keep them safe from predators. In time, the descendants of *Plateosaurus,* such as *Diplodocus,* roamed in herds on the Jurassic plains. Dinosaurs were set to rule the Earth.

Coelophysis
(SEEL-oh-FIE-sis)

LIVED: 225–220 mya

PERIOD: Triassic

LOCALITY: USA

LENGTH: 3 m (10 ft)

DIET: Carnivore – ate smaller animals

Improved Legs

The synapsids had legs that stuck out sideways from the body but the dinosaurs had their legs tucked in beneath the body. This meant that they could stand upright and move quickly, and also breathe more easily. This design feature was one of the most important reasons for the dinosaurs' dominance.

IMPROVED HIPS: Hips were strengthened by the joining of some of the hip vertebrae.

IMPROVED THIGHS: The head of the thigh bone turned inwards to slot into a strong hip socket.

IMPROVED KNEES AND ANKLES: These each had a simple hinge joint, which made them stronger.

RIGHT: The modern-day rhinoceros shares the straight leg position of the dinosaurs.

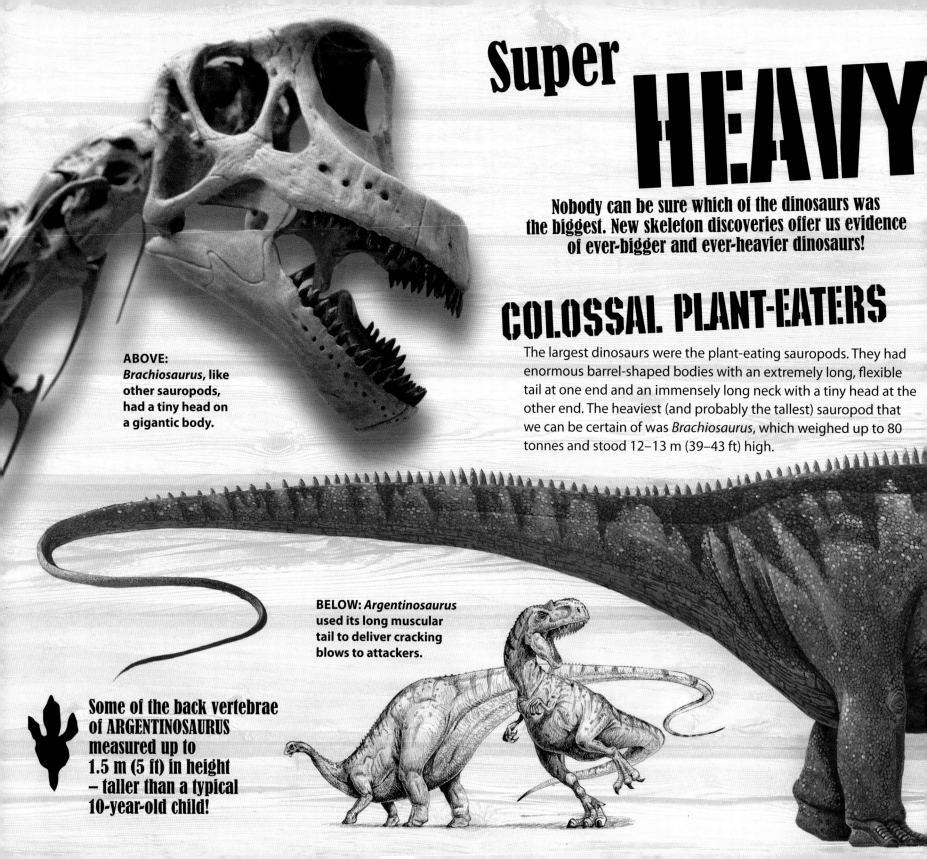

Super HEAVY

Nobody can be sure which of the dinosaurs was the biggest. New skeleton discoveries offer us evidence of ever-bigger and ever-heavier dinosaurs!

ABOVE:
Brachiosaurus, like other sauropods, had a tiny head on a gigantic body.

COLOSSAL PLANT-EATERS

The largest dinosaurs were the plant-eating sauropods. They had enormous barrel-shaped bodies with an extremely long, flexible tail at one end and an immensely long neck with a tiny head at the other end. The heaviest (and probably the tallest) sauropod that we can be certain of was *Brachiosaurus*, which weighed up to 80 tonnes and stood 12–13 m (39–43 ft) high.

BELOW: *Argentinosaurus* used its long muscular tail to deliver cracking blows to attackers.

Some of the back vertebrae of ARGENTINOSAURUS measured up to 1.5 m (5 ft) in height – taller than a typical 10-year-old child!

WEIGHTS

RIGHT: The fossilized tracks of a massive sauropod, which were found in Bolivia.

Colossal Contenders

The longest neck vertebra ever found was 1.2 m (4 ft) and belonged to *Sauroposeidon*. Fossils of two other sauropods, *Argentinosaurus* and *Supersaurus*, suggest that these beasts may have reached amazing lengths of 40 m (131 ft).

Possibly the biggest of all sauropods was a giant called *Amphicoelias*. Only part of one bone was discovered, and then lost again. Some scientists have calculated that this dinosaur was up to 60 m (197 ft) long and weighed up to a colossal 150 tonnes. This is as heavy as 25 elephants, easily making it king of the heavyweights!

ABOVE: A paleontologist works on the enormous neck vertebrae of a sauropod.

LEFT: Sauropods like this *Diplodocus* had long tails to balance their great necks.

THE BIG EASY

One reason the sauropods were so huge is because the bigger a creature is, the less likely it is to get eaten by a predator. Elephants, the largest land animals today, are so big that they are rarely threatened by lions. Sauropods also roamed the land in herds or family groups which gave them even greater protection against meat-eaters.

Sauropods didn't need to waste much energy moving around to find plants, as there was so much food available high up. They used their simple teeth to grab soft leaves from treetops. Some sauropods, such as *Diplodocus*, could also use their long necks to sweep across the ground in search of low-growing plants.

DIPLODOCUS

In the vast Jurassic landscape roamed a creature so enormous it dwarfed everything in its path.

The longest complete dinosaur skeleton that has been found is of *Diplodocus*, measuring a mighty 28 m (92 ft). To reach such an incredible size, after hatching from an egg not much bigger than a grapefruit, *Diplodocus* and other sauropods had to grow extremely quickly. *Apatosaurus*, for example, had a maximum growth rate of almost 5.5 tonnes per year!

The thick legs of DIPLODOCUS needed to support its massive shoulder bones and huge hips. They were built for strength, not speed.

DIPLODOCUS holds the record for the longest tail, at a staggering 13 m (42 ½ ft).

Monster Movers

The amazing length of *Diplodocus* has led scientists to question how this dinosaur moved and fed. Because it was so heavy, some early scientists though that it could only have moved if supported by water. We now know this isn't true. Some current scientists believe *Diplodocus* could raise itself up on its massive hind legs to reach high trees. What is known is that these sauropods protected each other by living in herds, which was especially useful for the young ones.

The frame of the mighty DIPLODOCUS dwarfs a man. This sauropod is the longest complete skeleton ever found.

WARNING!

DIPLODOCUS was the longest of the land dinosaurs. Much of its length was taken up by its incredible whip-like tail which could inflict nasty blows on enemies.

DIPLODOCUS
(Di-PLOD-o-kus)

LIVED: 155–145 mya

PERIOD: Jurassic

LOCALITY: USA

LENGTH: 28 m (92 ft)

WEIGHT: 10–16 tonnes

DIET: Herbivore – ate conifers and other leaves

Open crate with care. FRAGILE EGG INSIDE!

Dinosaur Action Zone

• To open the crate, press the SPACEBAR on your keyboard.

• To hatch the *Diplodocus* egg, press the UP direction key on your keyboard.

• To make the *Diplodocus* hatchling walk, press the DOWN direction key.

• Use the LEFT and RIGHT direction keys on your keyboard to make the *Diplodocus* change direction.

Flesh-eating
KiLLiNG MACHiNES

Which was the biggest carnivore? It was once thought to be Tyrannosaurus, but then a second, even mightier meat-eater was discovered...

BRUTAL BiTES

Tyrannosaurus, was once believed to be the largest meat-eater, at around 12.5 m (41 ft) long. But in 1994 it was pushed into second place when a huge and almost complete skeleton of the astonishing *Giganotosaurus* was unearthed. This powerful monster may have reached a length of just over 14 m (46 ft). It had enormous jaws in a 1.8 m- (6 ft-) long skull. Other heavyweight contenders are *Carcharodontosaurus* and *Tyrannotitan*, both relatives of *Giganotosaurus*.

Crushing and Slicing

Tyrannosaurus's long, pointed teeth were used in an open-mouthed charge against its prey. These powerful weapons were serrated (saw-edged) and could crush bones and tear out big chunks of flesh.

The teeth of *Giganotosaurus* were narrower and more curved. They were also serrated to slice through meat, probably after the victim had died. At 20 cm (8 in) long, they made deadly weapons.

Giganotosaurus
(GI-ga-NOH-toe-SORE-us)

LIVED: 112–90 mya

PERIOD: Cretaceous

LOCALITY: Argentina

LENGTH: 14 m (46 ft)

WEIGHT: 7–8 tonnes

DIET: Carnivore – ate any other animals it chose

GiGANOTOSAURUS VS TYRANNOSAURUS

The two heaviest meat-eating dinosaurs were *Giganotosaurus* and *Tyrannosaurus*. As we have seen, *Giganotosaurus* was probably a bit bigger (if a little slimmer), but they were both enormous, two-legged killing machines. *Giganotosaurus* lived earlier in the Cretaceous than *Tyrannosaurus*, and in South America. *Tyrannosaurus* lived in North America. Although *Giganotosaurus* had short arms, they were long enough for it to grab its prey with its three-fingered hands that ended in sharp claws. The short-armed *Tyrannosaurus* could never do this. *Tyrannosaurus* had the bigger brain, however – the brain of *Giganotosaurus* was the size and shape of a banana!

LEFT: Perhaps the largest predator ever to stalk the earth, *Giganotosaurus* terrorized the South American landscape around 95 million years ago.

BELOW: The massive skull of *Carcharodontosaurus*, a giant meat-eater from North Africa. Seen next to a man's skull, it is clear that this dinosaur could have easily swallowed a human whole.

CARCHARODONTOSAURUS was first discovered in 1920, but the fossils were destroyed by bombing during the Second World War. This giant predator remained lost until 1996, when scientists unearthed an even larger skull!

Micro MONSTERS

Some dinosaurs were tiny. Because their bones didn't fossilize very easily, only a few of these small species are well-known.

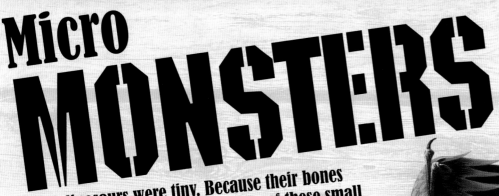

Scientists found a COMPSOGNATHUS fossil with the bones of an even smaller COMPSOGNATHUS in its stomach cavity. Was this tiny dinosaur a cannibal?

RIGHT: *Microraptor* takes the crown for smallest dinosaur.

BELOW: A tiny *Mussaurus* skeleton, the smallest ever found.

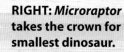

Microraptor
(MY-crow-RAP-tor)

LIVED: 130–122 mya

PERIOD: Cretaceous

LOCALITY: China

LENGTH: 55–75 cm (22–30 in)

DIET: Carnivore – ate small animals

TINY FINDS

The tiniest dinosaur ever found was a fossil named *Mussaurus*, or "Mouse Lizard". It was just 18 cm (7 in) long and was thought at the time to be the smallest species of dinosaur. However, scientists now believe it to be the skeleton of a baby prosauropod – in time it might have grown to reach a weight of more than 120 kg (265 lb)!

A better candidate for smallest dinosaur is *Microraptor*, discovered in China. It lived in the Cretaceous period, was 55–75 cm (22–30 in) long and had large flight feathers on its front and back legs. Scientists believe it spent its time in trees, jumping and gliding from branch to branch. It may also have flapped both pairs of legs like wings, in an early attempt to fly.

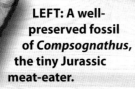

LEFT: A well-preserved fossil of *Compsognathus*, the tiny Jurassic meat-eater.

RIGHT and BELOW: Dinosaur eggs were amazingly small considering how large the dinosaurs inside would become.

BABY DINOSAURS

It is not surprising that the discoverers of the *Mussaurus* fossil thought at first that it was a new species of dinosaur. As we have seen, it would have grown up to become a prosauropod plant-eating dinosaur, rather like *Riojasaurus*. But even large sauropods laid surprisingly small eggs. A 30 m- (100 ft-) long female might lay eggs 30 cm (1 ft) long and 25 cm (10 in) wide – just think how tiny the baby would be compared to the adults!

It is now known that young dinosaurs grew very rapidly. Eggs came in all shapes and sizes, and had hard, brittle shells. A few fossilized eggs have contained babies' bones. Fossilized eggs, embryos and mud nests help us to learn about the dinosaurs and their way of life, from their growth and size to how they lived in groups.

Mini Meat-eater

Compsognathus was a tiny chicken-sized dinosaur from the Jurassic period. It caught small animals such as lizards and insects. Lightly built with hollow bones, its neck was long and flexible, and it could run quickly on its hind legs, using its tail for balance.

This dinosaur had big eyes and strong claws. Its nostrils were at the tip of a long nose, which suggests it had a strong sense of smell for sniffing out prey. Though not very strong, its jaws could clamp shut quickly to impale a victim on its small, sharp teeth.

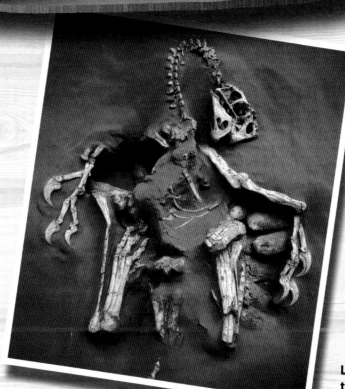

In 1869, the first complete fossilized dinosaur eggs were discovered in France, and were thought at the time to belong to a huge crocodile! They are now known to have been laid by the sauropod HYPSELOSAURUS.

LEFT: This *Oviraptor* appears to have died protecting its eggs.

Tough GUYS

Two groups of dinosaurs, the stegosaurs and ankylosaurs, protected themselves from predators with vicious body armour – including spines, spikes and clubs.

Even the eyelids of EUOPLOCEPHALUS were part of its armour. Made of bone, they shielded its eyes from slashing, attacking claws.

AWESOME ARMOUR

The best protected dinosaurs were the stegosaurs and the ankylosaurs. These plant-eaters needed all the help they could get to protect themselves against the vicious meat-eaters. They evolved a thick skin, sharp bony plates and spiked or clubbed tails that could deliver a deadly blow.

Stegosaurus was one of the biggest of the plated dinosaurs. It had a double row of thick bony plates along its back from head to tail, the largest of which was 61 cm (2 ft) tall. Its skin was covered with hard bony discs and two pairs of spikes at the end of its tail protected it from carnivores such as *Allosaurus*.

LEFT: *Allosaurus* would have risked a serious injury from the spiked tail of *Stegosaurus* in its search for food.

ABOVE: *Gastonia* was like an armoured tank. Predators would have to flip it over to get at its soft belly.

LEFT: Like *Stegosaurus*, a spiky porcupine uses its tail for defence.

ARMED TO THE TEETH

The real tough guys were the ankylosaurs who used their impressive armour to protect themselves against attack. They had sheets of bone protecting skull, neck and back, just as bony plates protect crocodiles' backs today. Their bodies were often covered with horns and spikes. When attacked, their strategy was a combination of active and passive defence.

A spiky species such as *Gastonia* used passive defence techniques. It would squat on the ground and rely on its armour to keep it safe, rather like today's armadillo. A club-tailed species like *Euoplocephalus* used active defence – it would try to disable its attacker with a blow from its tail.

ABOVE: Like Gastonia, an armadillo uses armour for passive defence.

Gastonia
(Gas-TONE-ee-uh)

LIVED: 125 mya

PERIOD: Cretaceous

LOCALITY: USA

LENGTH: 6.1 m (20 ft)

DIET: Herbivore – ate leaves and ferns

Tails of Defence

Some dinosaurs had devastating counter-attacking weapons – their tails. The tail of *Euoplocephalus* (below) was around 2.5 m (8 ft) in length, and ended with a massive club composed of two fused bones weighing up to 30 kg (66 lb). A single blow to the legs from this deadly body armour could crush bones, fatally injuring a predator such as *Tyrannosaurus*.

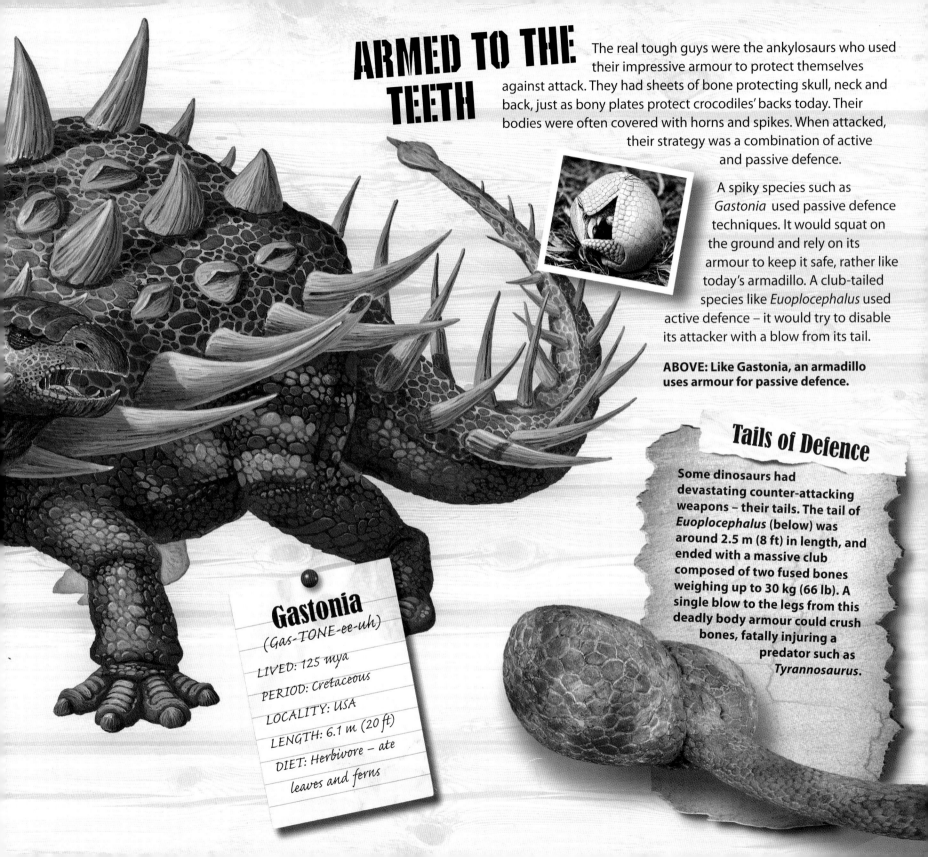

STEGOSAURUS

The bony plates on the back of the STEGOSAURUS were big and heavy – but what were they used for?

fossil of *Stegosaurus* skull

size and position of brain

Bearing in mind that STEGOSAURUS was the size of a truck, it is amazing that it managed to get by with such a small brain.

1. BACK OFF!

If *Stegosaurus* was threatened by predators, the blood vessels in its plates may have filled with blood, turning them a bright red. This might have been enough to scare off attackers.

2. HEATING UP, COOLING DOWN

The blood flowing through these plates may have been warmed by the sun and then pumped through the body of the *Stegosaurus* to heat it up. When the dinosaur became too hot, it could turn away from the sun to cool down.

3. ATTRACTING A MATE

The female *Stegosaurus* may have flushed her plates with blood to show males that she was ready to mate.

4. MY SPACE!

Just as male deer use their antlers to ward off rivals, so *Stegosaurus* may have used its flushing back plates to stop other males taking over its territory.

5. SOMETHING IN COMMON

Both male and female *Stegosaurus* may have used their back plates to show each other that they were the same species.

STEGOSAURUS was armed with four deadly tail spikes. Each around 90 cm (3 ft) long, they could inflict serious damage.

STEGOSAURUS
(STEG-oh-SORE-us)

LIVED: 155–145 mya

PERIOD: Jurassic

LOCALITY: USA

LENGTH: 9 m (29 ½ ft)

DIET: A herbivore – ate low-growing plants

Dinosaur Action Zone

- To open the crate, press the SPACEBAR on your keyboard.

- To make the *Stegosaurus* search for food, press the UP direction key.

- To make it prepare for battle, press the DOWN direction key.

Open crate with extreme caution. DANGEROUS BEAST INSIDE!

Sprinters and PLODDERS

Fossilized skeletons and dinosaur tracks give us clues as to how fast dinosaurs moved. Some could reach alarming speeds, while others were real plodders.

BUiLT FOR SPEED

Fast dinosaurs had light bones, streamlined bodies and two long legs. Ornithomimids, or "ostrich dinosaurs", such as *Gallimimus* and *Struthiomimus,* had these features. Like ostriches, they ran on two legs, had toothless beaks, and were omnivores, feeding on plants and insects. Unlike ostriches, they were featherless, had long tails for balance, and grasping arms. Ostriches can run at speeds of up to 70 kph (43 mph). *Gallimimus* might well have been just as fast.

RIGHT: The powerful back legs of *Gallimimus* were designed for quick sprinting.

Gallimimus
(GAL-ee-MY-mus)

LIVED: 74–70 mya

PERIOD: Cretaceous

LOCALITY: Mongolia

LENGTH: 5.5 m (18 ft)

DIET: Omnivore – ate plants and insects

Swift and Deadly

Velociraptor (meaning "speedy thief") had a light, streamlined body and long legs. Its stiff tail acted as a counter-balance when sprinting and allowed the dinosaur to turn quickly. This deadly predator combined speed and agility with needle-sharp teeth and killer claws.

Some scientists think *Velociraptors* hunted in packs. It is estimated that a pack could tear a human apart in under 30 seconds!

QUICK GETAWAY

Were any meat-eaters as speedy as the ostrich dinosaurs? Possibly *Velociraptor*, which had to catch its prey by running it down. Other fast dinosaurs were *Hypsilophodon* and the little *Coelophysis* – both plant-eaters designed for a quick getaway. Animals that rely on running to escape death are often very fast!

ABOVE: The legs of the sauropods looked much like those of elephants today.

THE PLODDERS

Which dinosaurs were the plodders? The sauropods moved the slowest, at about 6 kph (3.5 mph). Other dinosaurs that did not rely on speed to escape predators were the armoured varieties, such as *Hylaeosaurus*. Although they could probably gallop quite quickly for short distances, like a rhinoceros, they were not afraid to stand still and confront a predator. They relied on their heavy armour to protect them rather than on speed to escape.

RIGHT: The enormous back leg bones of *Diplodocus*.

Mighty Weight

Sauropods, such as *Brachiosaurus*, had four massive legs that supported their shoulders and hips like pillars. Their feet looked like those of elephants, and it is very probable that, like elephants, they had thick, soft pads under the back of each foot. Like the heels of shoes, these pads would keep the heels of the feet off the ground so that the dinosaur would not have to lift them at every step. This would save the dinosaur a lot of energy.

A fossil from Mongolia revealed a massive pair of 2.5m- (8ft-) forearms, with 25cm- (10in-) claws. Named DEINOCHEIRUS (meaning "terrible hands"), experts believe the bones may have come from an ornithomimid, probably the fastest group of dinosaurs.

ABOVE: *Velociraptor* was a fast and ferocious predator.

Scary ODDBALLS

Dinosaurs reigned supreme on land, but not in the water or the air. Awesome reptiles such as plesiosaurs and ichthyosaurs swam in the prehistoric seas. In the air were flying reptiles called pterosaurs.

ABOVE: The mighty *Quetzalcoatlus* was king of the Cretaceous skies.

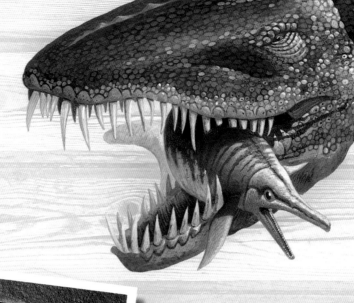

ABOVE: *Liopleurodon*, perhaps the largest predator ever.

FEARSOME FLYERS

The pterosaurs, or winged reptiles, lived alongside dinosaurs throughout the Triassic, Jurassic and Cretaceous periods. Instead of feathers, they had a sheet of very thin skin that stretched from the long fourth finger to the body and the back legs, acting as a wing. Flying animals need extremely lightweight bodies and the pterosaurs had hollow bones, even thinner than those of birds today. They were probably also warm-blooded, keeping their bodies at a constant temperature.

The first pterosaur ever discovered was *Pterodactylus*. It is also the earliest one known and lived in the Triassic period, 225 million years ago. The smallest known pterosaur is the Jurassic sparrow-sized *Anurognathus*.

RIGHT: A complete *Pterodactylus* fossil.

Toothy Record

The South American *Pterodaustro* holds the record for number of teeth, at between 500 and 1,000! It probably used these to filter-feed on plankton, like flamingos do.

MONSTERS OF THE DEEP

Liopleurodon
(LIE-oh-PLOO-ro-don)

LIVED: 160–155 mya

PERIOD: Jurassic

LOCALITY: UK and France

LENGTH: 25 m (82 ft)

WEIGHT: 100–150 tonnes

DIET: Carnivore – ate any large living thing

Under water, the greatest predator was the plesiosaur, *Liopleurodon*. Plesiosaurs breathed air and used paddle-like limbs to swim. *Liopleurodon* lived during the Jurassic period and may have weighed up to 150 tonnes. It reached 25 m (82 ft) in length – the head itself was 5 m (16 ft) long! It had nostrils on its skull which means that, like modern-day sharks, it may have found its food by smell. It would have eaten giant turtles and other plesiosaurs.

The ichthyosaurs were giant reptiles that looked like fish and dolphins. Among the biggest was *Shonisaurus*, which was at least 15 m (49 ft) long. This reptile swam like a shark, using its forked tail to propel it as fast as 40 kph (25 mph) through the water to catch its prey of ammonites (shelled creatures), fish and even the odd pterosaur.

OPHTHALMOSAURUS was an ichthyosaur with enormous eyes, 10 cm (4 in) across! These helped it to spot its prey in the deep, dark ocean.

EXTREME CROCODILES!

Deinosuchus and *Sarcosuchus* both lived in the Cretaceous period and are the biggest crocodiles ever found. *Deinosuchus* had a skull of nearly 2 m (6 ½ ft) long filled with razor-sharp teeth. It was well-equipped to seize hadrosaurs and even large carnivores that came close to the water's edge. It would have behaved like today's crocodiles – approaching its prey unseen and then lunging out to pull it into the water.

RIGHT: The 110 million-year-old skull of a *Sarcosuchus* crocodile dwarfs the skull of the modern-day Orinoco crocodile.

QUETZALCOATLUS

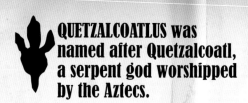

QUETZALCOATLUS was named after Quetzalcoatl, a serpent god worshipped by the Aztecs.

This fierce-looking giant of the sky would cast a terrifying shadow on the landscape as it glided on the winds.

Soaring overhead, the *Quetzalcoatlus* was the biggest pterosaur and the largest flying creature of all time. With a wingspan of up to 12 m (39 ft), it was the size of a small plane. It had hollow bones and weighed just 100 kg (220 lb). Unlike birds, *Quetzalcoatlus* had no feathers, but could fold its wings back over its body when it was not flying. It had a sharp claw on each thumb, like a bat. It may have slept like a bat does, too, hanging upside-down and holding on with its feet.

Giant Glider

Quetzalcoatlus was not a great flier, and relied on winds to help it soar and glide. On the end of its long neck was a huge head made up mostly of its great beak. It used this mighty beak to snap up invertebrates such as crabs and molluscs, and possibly fish.

The mighty head of QUETZALCOATLUS measured an amazing 2 m (6 ½ ft). Its neck was even longer, at 3 m (10 ft).

WARNING!

This strange and monstrous creature swooped out of the sky to snatch up prey and gobble it down.

QUETZALCOATLUS
(KWET-zal-co-AT-lus)

LIVED: 84–65 mya

PERIOD: Cretaceous

LOCALITY: USA

WINGSPAN: 12 m (39 ft)

WEIGHT: 100 kg (220 lb)

DIET: Carnivore – ate invertebrates and fish

Open crate with extreme caution. FLYING REPTILE INSIDE!

Dinosaur Action Zone

- To open the crate, press the SPACEBAR on your keyboard.
- To make the *Quetzalcoatlus* hunt for fish, press the DOWN direction key.
- To make it land, press the LEFT direction key.
- To make it take off again, press the RIGHT direction key.

Ferocious BEASTS

Terrifying giants such as SPINOSAURUS used their sheer size to overpower their victims. Smaller carnivores combined speed with razor-sharp fangs and claws for deadly attacks.

TERRIBLE CLAWS!

The clawed dinosaurs, such as *Velociraptor*, *Deinonychus* and *Utahraptor*, were lethal hunters. They were small but made up for this with their vicious claws, their great speed and by hunting in packs. *Deinonychus* (meaning "terrible claw") had three claws on each of its back feet. The claw on the second toe was enlarged to form a deadly, ripping blade. On the *Utahraptor* this claw was 30 cm (12 in) long!

When these dinosaurs ran on their hind legs, this special claw was held clear of the ground. When they caught up with their prey, the claw swung down to slice through the victim. Finally, the dinosaur's strong jaws and serrated teeth tore into the prey and the feeding frenzy began.

ABOVE: *Deinonychus* was an agile hunter with an enlarged claw for slicing.

Fossilized skeletons of VELOCIRAPTOR and PROTOCERATOPS were found locked in lethal combat in the Gobi Desert, 80 million years after their deaths.

Dinosaur Sails

Why dinosaurs like *Spinosaurus* had spiny sails on their backs is unclear, but one reason might have been to regulate body temperature. In the early morning sun, the blood in the sail would warm up, helping to heat the rest of the dinosaur's body – like a stegosaur's plates.

When the creature was too hot, it could turn away from the sun and the heat in the sail would radiate away. The sail might also have been brightly coloured to attract mates or repel rivals.

ABOVE: Like this crocodile, *Spinosaurus* had huge jaws for grabbing its prey.

Spinosaurus
(SPINE-oh-SORE-us)

LIVED: 95–70 mya

PERIOD: Cretaceous

LOCALITY: North Africa

LENGTH: 18 m (59 ft)

DIET: A carnivore – ate large fish and other dinosaurs

THE DEADLY SPINOSAURUS

One of the most ferocious dinosaurs that ever existed, *Spinosaurus* was also one of the most spectacular. Along its back were long, bony spines, 1.8 m (6 ft) in length, that supported a large sail of skin. At up to 18 m (59 ft) long, it was probably longer and certainly more agile than *Tyrannosaurus* or *Giganotosaurus*.

Like the clawed dinosaurs, *Spinosaurus* walked and ran on two legs, but unlike them it probably hunted alone, using its size and ambush tactics to catch its prey. Its 2m- (6.5 ft-) long skull had crocodile-like jaws with long, sharp teeth. Its prey probably consisted of large fish, but it would also have used its enormous jaws to kill other large dinosaurs.

The original German fossil specimen of SPINOSAURUS was destroyed by an air raid on Berlin in the Second World War.

Power PACKS

Small but lethal, carnivorous dinosaurs such as DEINONYCHUS roamed in deadly packs looking for lone, old or sick dinosaurs to attack.

TEAM TACTICS

Huge but lumbering plant-eaters had neither the strength nor the weapons to protect themselves from the packs of vicious meat-eaters that roamed in search of a meal. Dinosaurs such as *Deinonychus* were quick, agile, smart and lethal. They would surround a victim and leap on its back, tearing at its flesh. These fearsome predators used their razor-sharp curved claws to slash through tough skin and muscle and would continue their attack until the prey died from blood loss or exhaustion.

Bony struts reinforced the tail of DEINONYCHUS so that it could hold its tail still when running. This helped it to balance.

Deinonychus
(Die-NON-ee-kus)

LIVED: 110 mya

PERIOD: Cretaceous

LOCALITY: USA

LENGTH: 3 m (10 ft)

DIET: A carnivore – ate large herbivores when hunting in packs

RIGHT: Lions blend into the landscape. It is likely that dinosaur pack-hunters also matched the colours of their environment.

Clever Camouflage

Dinosaur predators that hunted in packs would have been camouflaged so they could creep up on their prey without being spotted. Their skin would have been pale beige, grey or brown, similar to those of today's hunters such as wolves and lions.

A leopard's spots and a tiger's stripes make them nearly impossible to see when lying in wait. In the same way, the coloured patterns on a dinosaur's body would have broken up its outline and made it harder to spot.

ABOVE: A *Tenontosaurus* is attacked by a savage pack of *Deinonychus*.

Big HEADS

The horned dinosaurs used their heads when it came to protection, self-defence and display. Their thick skulls and deadly horns helped them to fight off the fiercest attackers.

Fancy Headgear

Many hadrosaurs had tall head crests. The crests of males were probably brightly coloured and used both to attract females and threaten other males during courtship.

Some of the crests were hollow and may have been used to make different loud noises, or "songs". *Parasaurolophus* (left) had perhaps the strangest crest of all – it was shaped like a trombone and was nearly 1.8 m (6 ft) long.

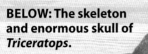

BELOW: The skeleton and enormous skull of *Triceratops*.

HORNED FIGHTER

One of the largest of the horned dinosaurs, *Triceratops* (meaning "three-horn face") used its long sharp horns as deadly weapons. It would have fought fierce battles with predators such as *Tyrannosaurus*, and even other rival males. *Triceratops* skulls have been found with *Tyrannosaurus* teeth marks in them. Other *Triceratops* fossils show scars from wounds made by the horns of rival males. Careful study of the way these scars have healed shows scientists that the *Triceratops* often survived these nasty wounds to fight another day.

RIGHT: With its three sharp horns, *Triceratops* was a good match for *Tyrannosaurus*.

BELOW: Two male *Pentaceratops* prepare to lock horns.

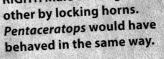

RIGHT: Male deer fight each other by locking horns. *Pentaceratops* would have behaved in the same way.

Impressing the Ladies

Dinosaurs such as *Pentaceratops* and *Pachycephalosaurus* used their heads for fighting and to attract a mate.

Heterodontosaurus males had tusks like a wild boar's, while *Spinosaurus* may have used the huge crest on his back to attract females or to ward off other males. *Stegosaurus* may have used his bony plates, and *Deinonychus* his long curved claws, for the same reasons.

Incredibly, the mighty head belonging to PACHYCEPHALOSAURUS housed a brain not much bigger than an apple!

THE BONE HEADS

The only part of *Pachycephalosaurus* that has been found is its massive skull. The back of this dinosaur's head was covered with bony knobs and it had short spikes on top of the snout. All the evidence from fossils suggests that these dinosaurs used their thick heads for butting. Their spines were strengthened with bony rods, and the joint between the skull and the neck was designed to absorb the shock from a head butt.

It used to be thought that the male *Pachycephalosaurus* fought for a mate by ramming a rival's head. However, scientists have since discovered that its skull could not survive a blow from an equally strong head. It seems more likely that it used its head to ram predators. Although not very fast, *Pachycephalosaurus* was the length of a large car – even *Tyrannosaurus* would have been hurt if a dinosaur of this size crashed into it head first!

RIGHT: The skull of *Pachycephalosaurus* had a huge dome of bone.

PENTACERATOPS

It may have been a plant eater but the five-horned PENTACERATOPS had the weapons to fight off the meanest meat eater.

Pentaceratops (meaning "five-horn face") protected its head with two sharp horns above its eyes, one on its nose and two "spikes" that stuck out sideways from its cheeks. It also had a huge neck frill, which was studded with spikes along the edge and helped to protect its back. This fierce beast would charge at a predator to spike it with deadly, flesh-ripping horns.

Head to Head

Some scientists believe the skin covering *Pentaceratops*'s frill may have been brightly coloured. It is likely that both the male and female of this species used their coloured frills as a display to each other. The males may also have used them as a sign to rivals to stay away. If the display didn't work, the males would have fought each other head first.

PENTACERATOPS charged enemies with its horns, much like the modern-day rhinoceros does.

The largest dinosaur skull ever discovered belonged to PENTACERATOPS. It was more than 3 m (10 ft) long and consisted mainly of a huge bony frill.

The sharp beak of PENTACERATOPS would have been strong enough to snap the shin bone of many an enemy.

WARNING!

Sharp as a dagger, the horns above the eyes of PENTACERATOPS could measure up to 1 m (3 ft) in length.

PENTACERATOPS
(PEN-ta-SER-a-tops)

LIVED: 76–73 mya

PERIOD: Cretaceous

LOCALITY: USA

LENGTH: 8 m (26 ft)

SKULL LENGTH: 3 m (10 ft)

DIET: Herbivore – ate tough, low-lying plants

Open crates with extreme caution. HORNED BEASTS INSIDE!

Dinosaur Action Zone

- To open each crate, press the SPACEBAR on your keyboard.

- To see the *Pentaceratops* males threaten each other, press the UP direction key.

- To make them fight, press the DOWN direction key.

The Longest and the TALLEST

TALL STORIES

The tallest living mammal is the giraffe (above), which can reach up to 6 m (19 ½ ft). *Brachiosaurus*, standing at up to 13 m (42 ½ ft), was the tallest dinosaur. Its front legs were longer than its back legs, and it held its neck upright. These features suggest that, like a giraffe, it fed on leaves from the tops of trees.

Although *Brachiosaurus* and its relatives held their heads high, it is likely that the long necks of most giant sauropods were held horizontally. This would allow them to look for low-growing plants across great areas of land without using too much energy. Some scientists believed that *Sauroposeidon* fed in exactly this way, which means that it was very long rather than very tall.

LEFT: The upright *Brachiosaurus* is the tallest dinosaur that scientists can be sure of.

The sauropods were not only the heaviest ever land animals. Their incredibly long necks and tails mean that they also win prizes for the longest and the tallest of all the dinosaurs.

LEFT: The incredibly long tail of *Apatosaurus* counter-balanced its very long neck.

A Cracking Tail

The long tail of the *Diplodocus* may have been used like a whip against predators such as *Allosaurus*. However, the final two metres of the tail were very thin, not much more than 30 mm (1 in) thick, and striking predators might have damaged it.

It has been calculated that *Diplodocus* could move the tip of its tail at supersonic speeds. This would have made a loud cracking noise that might have been used to frighten off enemies. *Diplodocus* might also have moved its tail to communicate with members of the same species.

LEFT: A fossilized vertebra from the sauropod *Barosaurus*.

REACHING FOR THE STARS

It is likely that some sauropods, such as *Diplodocus* and *Mamenchisaurus*, could reach just as high or even higher than *Brachiosaurus* by rearing up on their back legs.

The rear legs of *Diplodocus* were bigger than its front legs, making its centre of gravity further back than that of *Brachiosaurus*. This could have allowed it to rear up on its back legs while using its tail to steady its body. The neck of *Diplodocus* was 8 m (26 ft) long, so its head could easily have reached the treetops.

The record for the longest neck-to-body ratio is held by a sauropod called ERKETU. Its neck, was 8 m (26 ft) long, twice the length of its body!

RIGHT: The gerenuk, a modern-day African antelope, rears up on its back legs to feed. Sauropods, like *Mamenchisaurus*, may well have fed in the same way.

In 2005, scientists announced the discovery of a stumpy-necked sauropod. BRACHYTRACHELOPAN had a neck shorter than its backbone, making it the shortest sauropod neck on record.

Long Necks

Although it couldn't reach as high as *Diplodocus*, the Chinese dinosaur *Mamenchisaurus* had a neck that was nearly 14 m (46 ft) long, the longest scientists are sure about. The neck consisted of 19 bones. These were hollow and light, making it possible for *Mamenchisaurus* to support its amazing length.

Sauroposeidon may have had an even longer neck. Although only four fossil bones have ever been found belonging to this dinosaur, they are all neck vertebrae. Each one is an incredible 1.2 m (4 ft) long.

LEFT: *Mamenchisaurus* takes the prize for the longest neck.

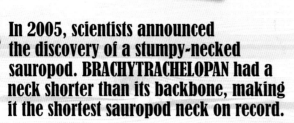
Mamenchisaurus
(Mah-MEN-chi-SORE-us)

LIVED: 155–145 mya

PERIOD: Jurassic

LOCALITY: China

LENGTH: 24 m (80 ft)

DIET: A herbivore – ate high-growing plants

Master-MINDS

There is no doubt that many dinosaurs got by with very little brain power, but just as with mammals living today, some groups were smarter than others.

CLEVER IS AS CLEVER DOES

How do scientists test an animal for intelligence? They look at its way of life or they measure the animal's brain and compare it to its body size. Animals that lead complicated lives need to be more intelligent than animals that lead simple lives. The sauropods were so enormous that they didn't need to worry about predators. They led simple lives and so had little brain power.

Large carnivores, such as *Tyrannosaurus,* needed to find their food, then catch it and kill it. Like most predators, they had forward-facing eyes so that they could judge distances. A bigger brain was needed for these complicated activities.

Fast-running carnivores, such as *Velociraptor,* needed even more intelligence as they hunted as a pack. They had to be able to communicate with other members of the group and react quickly to changing situations. *Toodon,* and other smaller carnivores, needed still greater brain power to stalk and then chase their prey.

ABOVE:
The skull of *Diplodocus.* The massive sauropods were pretty low on brain power.

A Question of Size?

The brain doesn't fossilize, so scientists have to estimate its size by making a cast of the inside of the skull. They then need to compare the brain size with the size of the dinosaur to get an idea of its intelligence. When scientists do this they get the same results as when looking at dinosaur lifestyles – the sauropods come bottom of the class and the smaller carnivores come top.

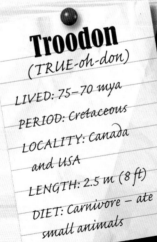

Troodon
(TRUE-oh-don)

LIVED: 75–70 mya

PERIOD: Cretaceous

LOCALITY: Canada and USA

LENGTH: 2.5 m (8 ft)

DIET: Carnivore – ate small animals

BIG BRAINS AND NO BRAINS!

Although *Troodon* takes the prize for smartest dinosaur, the biggest brain of any dinosaur probably belonged to the giant meat-eater, *Tyrannosaurus*. Its brain was about the size of a human's but when you think how much bigger its body was, that doesn't make it a master-mind!

Stegosaurus takes the prize for smallest brain. Its body was the size of a truck, but with a brain the size of a walnut, there wasn't much going on upstairs!

LEFT: *Troodon* **came top of the class for intelligence.**

It was once thought that STEGOSAURUS had a second brain. Paleontologists now realize that this "brain" was actually an enlarged nerve centre in the spinal cord, located in the hip area. It may have been used to control the hind legs and tail.

ABOVE: *Stegosaurus* **was no brain-box!**

GOLD STAR!

Top-of-the-class *Troodon* was a small dinosaur that stalked and chased agile prey. It had large, forward-facing eyes for judging distances, and big spaces in its nose, which means that it used smell to detect its food. Also, its brain was the biggest of any dinosaur, relative to its body size, and can be compared to that of a modern ostrich. However, this may not be such a huge compliment, given that there is a true story of an ostrich that got its head stuck in the fork of a tree.

LEFT: The modern-day ostrich can be compared to *Troodon* **in terms of intelligence.**

Test Your Brainpower!

Are you a *Troodon* **or an** *Apatosaurus* **when it comes to learning new facts? Once you've read this book from cover to cover, take this quiz and find out!**

Of course, you might need to check through the book again to refresh your memory. The answers can be found on the back page and you get 1 point for every question you answer correctly. No cheating!

1. **Which group of reptiles did the dinosaurs come from?**
   a. Archosaurs
   b. Mammal-like reptiles
   c. Synapsids
   d. Turtles

2. **When did the first dinosaurs appear?**
   a. Cretaceous
   b. Jurassic
   c. Permian
   d. Triassic

3. **Which is the smallest fossil dinosaur ever found?**
   a. Bee hummingbird
   b. *Compsognathus*
   c. *Microraptor*
   d. *Mussaurus*

4. **Which dinosaur had the longest neck vertebra?**
   a. *Brachiosaurus*
   b. *Diplodocus*
   c. *Giganotosaurus*
   d. *Sauroposeidon*

5. **Which dinosaur protected itself from meat-eating dinosaurs by hitting them with the bony club on its tail?**
   a. *Euoplocephalus*
   b. *Gastonia*
   c. *Huayangosaurus*
   d. *Stegosaurus*

6. **Which of the following could run the fastest?**
   a. *Hylaeosaurus*
   b. *Hypsilophodon*
   c. *Triceratops*
   d. *Tyrannosaurus*

7. **Which deadly carnivorous dinosaur had a large sail-like crest on its back?**
   a. *Deinonychus*
   b. *Ouranosaurus*
   c. *Spinosaurus*
   d. *Tyrannosaurus*

8. **Which of the following was the most intelligent?**
   a. *Argentinosaurus*
   b. *Iguanodon*
   c. *Troodon*
   d. *Tyrannosaurus*

9. **Which dinosaur had the thickest skull?**
   a. *Pachycephalosaurus*
   b. *Parasaurolophus*
   c. *Pentaceratops*
   d. *Prenocephale*

10. **What did** *Liopleurodon* **eat?**
    a. Birds
    b. Large reptiles
    c. Plankton
    d. Plants

11. **Which of the following is a dinosaur?**
    a. *Crocodilus*
    b. *Liopleurodon*
    c. *Mussaurus*
    d. *Quetzalcoatlus*

12. **Where is the Chicxulub Crater?**
    a. Majorca
    b. Mexico
    c. Monaco
    d. Mozambique

Extreme EATERS

Dinosaurs needed food for energy and they had some strange ways of making the most of their meals.

LEFT: Sauropods needed stomach stones to aid digestion.

RIGHT: The skull of a *Protoceratops* shows its sharp beak for slicing leaves and shoots.

HEAVY-DUTY EATING

The heaviest dinosaur, a sauropod such as *Brachiosaurus*, probably needed to eat about a tonne of plants every day! But its little peg-teeth were no good for chewing so to help it to process this tough plant food it swallowed stones (gastroliths). These stones sat in a special muscular stomach, called a gizzard, and helped the sauropod to digest the food by grinding it to a pulp. When the gastroliths became too smooth to work properly, they were belched out and replaced by new ones.

The smaller herbivores, such as *Hadrosaurus*, had good grinding teeth, while ceratopians, such as *Triceratops*, used their beaks to slice up plant food.

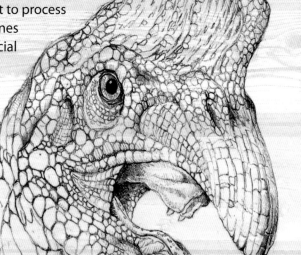

LEFT: *Oviraptor* used its powerful jaw and "teeth" to crush its food.

Grinders, Slicers and Crushers

A duck-billed dinosaur like *Edmontosaurus* used its beak to pull in plant food such as bark. Its jaw contained over 1,000 teeth used for grinding down the food.

Horned dinosaurs had sharp, narrow, toothless beaks rather like a parrot's (below). *Protoceratops* used its beak to slice off shoots and leaves. Further back in its mouth it had self-sharpening, scissor-like teeth that chopped and sliced food.

Although it had no proper teeth, the *Oviraptor* had two knobs that looked a bit like big teeth in the roof of its mouth. It used these to crush dinosaurs' eggs.

MEATY MOUTHFULS

Solo carnivores hunting for food would look out for easy prey such as the sick, the old or the young. The mighty *Giganotosaurus* probably hunted by ambushing its prey. It would hide in the thick trees until a slow-moving plant eater came by. Then it would crash into it and bite deep into its flesh. It probably filled up while it had the chance and could then last for days without eating.

Smaller predators had their own specialized weapons. *Deinonychus* and *Velociraptor* had lethal, swivelling claws, and most of the others, such as *Coelophysis* and *Troodon*, had grasping hands. Some hunted in packs, running down slower dinosaurs. Most of the predators had a well-developed sense of smell and binocular vision (forward facing) to spot prey at a distance.

Allosaurus
(AL-oh-SORE-us)

LIVED: 155–145 mya

PERIOD: Jurassic

LOCALITY: USA and Portugal

LENGTH: 12 m (39 ft)

DIET: Carnivore – ate other dinosaurs

DINOSAUR DROPPINGS

Coprolites (pieces of fossilized dung) may contain remains such as seeds, leaves, fish scales, teeth and bits of partially digested bone that tell us what dinosaurs liked to eat. Many coprolites are up to 40 cm (16 in) in diameter, and were probably deposited by sauropods like *Diplodocus*.

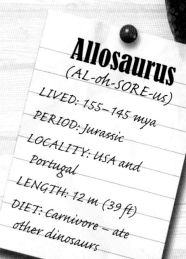

ABOVE: Coprolites provide interesting clues as to what dinosaurs ate.

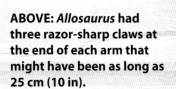

ABOVE: *Allosaurus* had three razor-sharp claws at the end of each arm that might have been as long as 25 cm (10 in).

TYRANNOSAURUS

The deadliest of all dinosaurs had dagger-like teeth and powerful jaws that could easily crush a victim's bones.

One of the heaviest meat-eating dinosaurs, *Tyrannosaurus* was an enormous, two-legged killing machine that roamed North America over 65 million years ago. *Tyrannosaurus*'s long, pointed, teeth had saw-like edges, which allowed them to slice through meat as easily as a kitchen knife.

Mighty Bites

Tyrannosaurus had tiny arms that were incapable of holding its victims securely, so it used its powerful neck muscles to rip out flesh with its mouth, swallowing it straight away. This dinosaur could easily crush tough matter, such as bones, and swallow the fragments. If any of its teeth were broken, new ones grew to replace them. Puncture wounds found in the bones of victims show that *Tyrannosaurus* sunk its teeth deep into the flesh and bones of its prey. A huge predator like this would need to eat the equivalent of three or four adult *Triceratops* per year (or 292 adult men)!

TYRANNOSAURUS had a massive jaw with 15 cm- (6 in-) serrated teeth. These could cause terrible flesh wounds and crush bones.

TYRANNOSAURUS would have used its hugely powerful neck to violently shake its victims to death.

It has been calculated that TYRANNOSAURUS normally chewed with a force of 1.35 tonnes – the equivalent of a pick-up truck on top of each tooth!

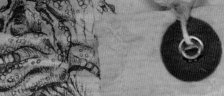

TYRANNOSAURUS

(Tie-RAN-oh-SORE-us)

LIVED: 75–65 mya

PERIOD: Cretaceous

LOCALITY: USA

LENGTH: 12.5 m (41 ft)

DIET: Carnivore – ate other dinosaurs, alive or dead

Open crate with extreme caution. DEADLY PREDATOR INSIDE!

Dinosaur Action Zone

• To open the crate, press the SPACEBAR on your keyboard.

• To make the *Tyrannosaurus* walk, press the UP direction key.

• To make it angry, press the DOWN direction key.

Death and
EXTINCTION

For more than 160 million years the dinosaurs dominated the land, but around 65 million years ago they disappeared completely – and no one can be certain why this happened...

DEATH BY DEGREES

By the end of the Cretaceous period, there were fewer dinosaur species and these were dominated by herbivores such as *Edmontosaurus* and *Triceratops*, and some bone-headed dinosaurs like *Pachycephalosaurus*. Ostrich dinosaurs such as *Ornithomimus* roamed the open areas and the sickle-clawed *Troodon* was common. While the dinosaurs were becoming fewer in variety, mammals were increasing.

Why did this happen? The climate was becoming wetter. Perhaps new rivers and swamps made it more difficult for the herbivores to reach fresh feeding ranges and so they began to die off. This would have affected the carnivores' food supply and their numbers would also have dropped. However, this does not explain the sudden disappearance of the sea reptiles and the pterosaurs cruising the sky. What happened so quickly that large land animals had no time to adapt?

RIGHT: An *Edmontosaurus* lies dead in the sand.

LEFT: A skull belonging to *Edmontosaurus*, one of the last surviving dinosaurs.

ABOVE: The modern-day elephant shrew eats small invertebrates, as did mammal survivors from the age of dinosaurs.

The Survivors

Apart from birds, the most successful survivors from the dinosaur age were the small mammals such as *Zalambdalestes* from Mongolia or *Megazostrodon* from Lesotho.

Both were long-nosed mammals with large eyes and a mouth of sharp teeth. *Didelphodon*, a marsupial related to opossums, was one of the biggest mammals of the Cretaceous period.

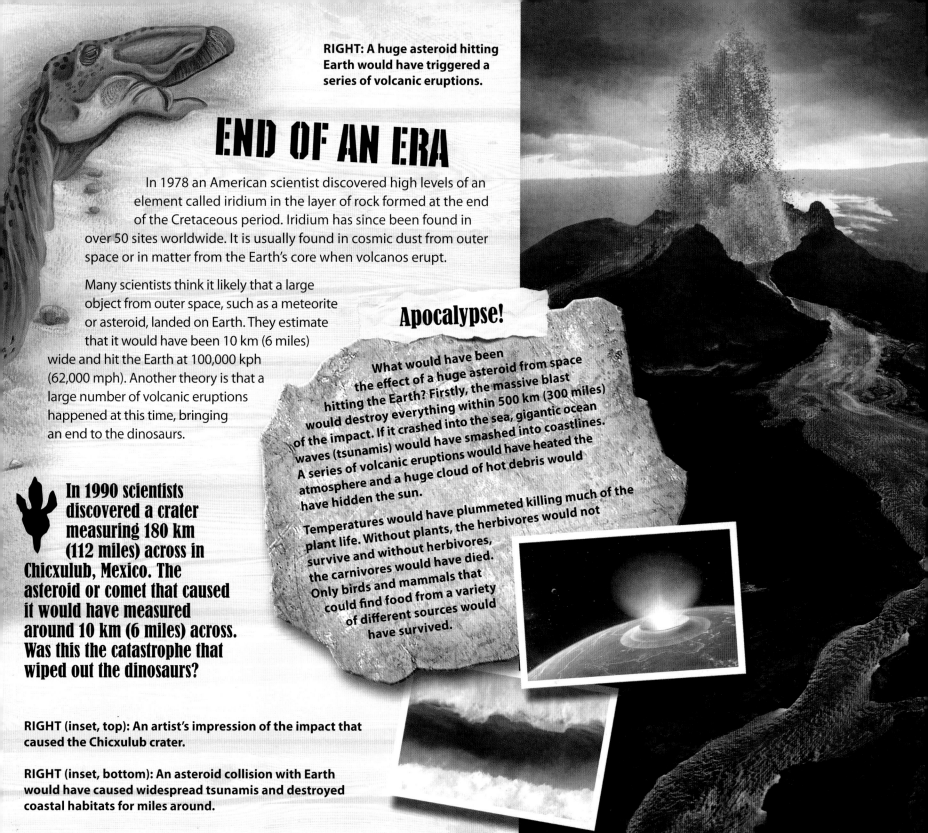

RIGHT: A huge asteroid hitting Earth would have triggered a series of volcanic eruptions.

END OF AN ERA

In 1978 an American scientist discovered high levels of an element called iridium in the layer of rock formed at the end of the Cretaceous period. Iridium has since been found in over 50 sites worldwide. It is usually found in cosmic dust from outer space or in matter from the Earth's core when volcanos erupt.

Many scientists think it likely that a large object from outer space, such as a meteorite or asteroid, landed on Earth. They estimate that it would have been 10 km (6 miles) wide and hit the Earth at 100,000 kph (62,000 mph). Another theory is that a large number of volcanic eruptions happened at this time, bringing an end to the dinosaurs.

In 1990 scientists discovered a crater measuring 180 km (112 miles) across in Chicxulub, Mexico. The asteroid or comet that caused it would have measured around 10 km (6 miles) across. Was this the catastrophe that wiped out the dinosaurs?

Apocalypse!

What would have been the effect of a huge asteroid from space hitting the Earth? Firstly, the massive blast would destroy everything within 500 km (300 miles) of the impact. If it crashed into the sea, gigantic ocean waves (tsunamis) would have smashed into coastlines. A series of volcanic eruptions would have heated the atmosphere and a huge cloud of hot debris would have hidden the sun.

Temperatures would have plummeted killing much of the plant life. Without plants, the herbivores would not survive and without herbivores, the carnivores would have died. Only birds and mammals that could find food from a variety of different sources would have survived.

RIGHT (inset, top): An artist's impression of the impact that caused the Chicxulub crater.

RIGHT (inset, bottom): An asteroid collision with Earth would have caused widespread tsunamis and destroyed coastal habitats for miles around.

GLOSSARY

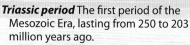

ammonites An extinct group of coiled shellfish, related to squid and octopuses, that teemed in Mesozoic seas.

amphibians Cold-blooded vertebrates that live on land but return to the water to breed. Living amphibians include frogs and newts.

ankylosaurs Armoured, plant-eating ornithischian dinosaurs.

archosaurs A major group of reptiles that includes dinosaurs, pterosaurs, thecodonts and crocodiles.

belemnites An extinct group of molluscs, with an internal shell.

carnivore A meat-eater.

cold-blooded Having a body temperature that rises and falls according to the outside temperature.

conifers A cone-bearing tree such as a yew or pine.

continent A large, continuous body of land, e.g. Africa.

coprolite Fossilized dung.

corals Sea animals, related to sea anemones, with tough outside skeletons, often forming reefs.

courtship display Behaviour used to attract a partner for reproduction.

Cretaceous period The third period of the Mesozoic era, lasting from 135 to 65 million years ago.

cycads Squat, palm-like plants, common in the Mesozoic era. Some have survived to the present day.

dinosaurs A great group of land-living reptiles with an upright stance that lived between 230 and 65 million years ago.

embryo An animal or plant in its earliest stages of development.

evolution The process by which one species gives rise to another by gradual changes in its characteristics over a period of time.

extinction The dying out of a species.

ferns Early non-flowering land plants, common in the Mesozoic era and surviving to the present day.

fossil The preserved remains of a once-living organism.

gastroliths Stomach stones used for grinding plant food.

ginkgo Also known as the maidenhair tree, its ancestors were very common in the Mesozoic era.

gizzard The muscular part of the stomach used to grind up food.

hadrosaurs Duck-billed dinosaurs which flourished in the Cretaceous period.

herbivore A plant-eater.

ichthyosaurs Sea reptiles of the Mesozoic era.

invertebrates Animals without a backbone.

iridium A metal found in meteorites and the earth's core.

Jurassic period The middle period of the Mesozoic era, lasting from 203 to 135 million years ago.

mammals Warm-blooded vertebrates that have hair and feed their young on milk.

marine Found in the sea.

Mesozoic era The period of time, 250–65 million years ago, containing the Triassic, Jurassic and Cretaceous periods, when the dinosaurs lived.

meteorite A meteor that lands on Earth.

molluscs A group of invertebrates, including snails, squid and octopuses.

MYA Million Years Ago.

omnivore An animal that eats both animals and plants.

ornithischians One of the two main groups of dinosaurs, in which the hips are similar to those of birds.

ornithomimids Fast-running, long-legged dinosaurs resembling ostriches.

paleontologist A special scientist who studies fossils.

Pangaea The supercontinent formed at the end of the Permian period when all the continents of the earth collided.

Permian The last period of the Palaeozoic era, from 295 to 250 million years ago.

plankton Microscopic organisms found in seas and lakes.

plesiosaurs Marine reptiles living in the Mesozoic era.

predator An animal that hunts and kills animals for its food.

prey An animal hunted or killed by another animal for food.

prosauropods Early plant-eating dinosaurs that lived from the late Triassic period to the early Jurassic period.

pterosaurs Flying reptiles that lived in the Mesozoic era and close relatives of the dinosaurs.

reptiles Cold-blooded, scaly vertebrates that usually lay eggs, such as crocodiles, snakes and lizards.

saurischians One of the two main groups of dinosaurs, in which the hips are similar to those of lizards.

sauropods Large, four-legged, plant-eating dinosaurs with enormous necks and tails.

scavenger An animal that feeds on dead organisms.

stegosaurs Plant-eating dinosaurs with bony plates or spines running down their backs and tails.

thecodonts An old-fashioned name for a group of Triassic reptiles that gave rise to crocodiles, dinosaurs, and probably flying reptiles (pterosaurs).

theropods A group of saurischian dinosaurs that includes nearly all the carnivores.

Triassic period The first period of the Mesozoic Era, lasting from 250 to 203 million years ago.

troodonts Small Cretaceous hunting dinosaurs.

tsunami A gigantic sea wave caused by a disturbance of the ocean floor, such as an earthquake.

vertebrae The bones of the spine.

vertebrates Animals with a backbone.

volcano An opening in the Earth's crust which expels gases and lava.

warm-blooded A warm-blooded animal uses its body chemistry to regulate its body temperature.